SOUTHWEST FLORIDA TRAVEL GUIDE

Exciting Things To Do In Southwest Florida

Bonita Green

Copyright © [2024] [Bonita Green]

Table of content

Chapter One: Discovering Southwest Florida

Introduction to Southwest Florida

Southwest Florida is a mesmerizing region renowned for its natural beauty, cultural diversity, and vibrant communities. As you embark on your journey through this enchanting destination, prepare to be captivated by its lush landscapes, pristine beaches, and rich history.

The coastline of Southwest Florida is adorned with powdery white sands that stretch for miles, inviting visitors to relax under the warm sun or take a leisurely stroll along the water's edge. From the tranquil shores of Sanibel Island to the bustling beaches of Naples, each coastal enclave offers its own unique charm and allure.

Inland, you'll discover a tapestry of verdant forests, meandering rivers, and tranquil lakes, providing endless opportunities for outdoor adventure. Whether you're kayaking through the peaceful waters of the Everglades, hiking along scenic nature trails, or birdwatching in one of the region's many wildlife preserves, Southwest Florida offers an abundance of recreational activities for nature enthusiasts of all ages.

Beyond its natural wonders, Southwest Florida boasts a rich cultural heritage that is reflected in its vibrant arts scene, eclectic cuisine, and colorful festivals. From the historic streets of downtown Fort Myers, where you can explore charming boutiques and art galleries, to the lively waterfront districts of Sarasota and Punta Gorda, where live music and entertainment abound, the region's cultural offerings are as diverse as they are captivating.

Throughout Southwest Florida, you'll also encounter a wealth of historic sites and landmarks that offer insight into the region's past, from the Calusa Indian mounds of Mound Key Archaeological State Park to the grand estates of the Gilded Age in Sarasota. These timeless treasures provide a glimpse into the rich tapestry of history that has shaped the character of Southwest Florida over the centuries.

As you immerse yourself in the beauty of Southwest Florida, you'll be greeted with warm hospitality and a sense of community that is as inviting as the sun-drenched landscapes that surround you. Whether you're savoring fresh seafood at a waterfront restaurant, attending a lively street festival, or simply enjoying a sunset stroll along the beach, you'll find that the beauty of Southwest Florida extends far beyond its natural scenery—it lies in the warmth and spirit of its people, who welcome visitors with open arms and open hearts.

Geography and Climate

Southwest Florida is a region of diverse geography and a subtropical climate that entices visitors and residents alike with its natural beauty and outdoor recreation opportunities.

Geography:

Spanning from the southern end of Tampa Bay to the edge of the Everglades, Southwest Florida is characterized by its mix of coastal areas, barrier islands, wetlands, and inland communities. The region is home to cities such as Sarasota, Fort Myers, Naples, and Punta Gorda, each offering its own distinct landscape and attractions.

The coastline of Southwest Florida is famous for its stunning beaches, including Siesta Key Beach, known for its powdery white sands, and Sanibel Island, renowned for its shelling opportunities. Barrier islands like Captiva and Gasparilla Island provide a natural buffer against storms and offer tranquil retreats for visitors seeking seclusion.

Inland, the landscape transitions into lush wetlands and forests, particularly in areas like the Everglades and the Big Cypress National Preserve. These pristine ecosystems are home to a rich diversity of wildlife, including alligators, manatees, and a multitude of bird species.

Climate:

Southwest Florida enjoys a subtropical climate characterized by warm temperatures, abundant sunshine, and distinct wet and dry seasons.

Summers in the region are hot and humid, with average temperatures ranging from the high 80s to low 90s Fahrenheit (around 31-34°C). Afternoon thunderstorms are common during the summer months, providing relief from the heat and nourishing the region's lush vegetation.

Winters in Southwest Florida are mild and pleasant, with average temperatures ranging from the mid-60s to low 70s Fahrenheit (around 18-23°C). This temperate climate makes the region a popular destination for "snowbirds" seeking to escape colder northern climates.

The wet season in Southwest Florida typically occurs from June through September, with the highest rainfall totals recorded during these months. Conversely, the dry season, which runs from October through May, experiences significantly less precipitation, creating ideal conditions for outdoor activities and tourism.

Overall, Southwest Florida's geography and climate combine to create an inviting environment for residents and visitors alike, offering a wealth of outdoor recreational opportunities, natural wonders, and year-round sunshine. Whether exploring its pristine beaches, venturing into its untamed wilderness areas, or enjoying its vibrant cultural scene, Southwest Florida provides a captivating destination for all who visit.

Biodiversity and Natural Wonders

Southwest Florida is home to a rich tapestry of biodiversity and natural wonders, encompassing diverse ecosystems that support a wide array of plant and animal species. From the lush wetlands of the Everglades to the pristine beaches and barrier islands along the Gulf Coast, the region is teeming with life and offers unparalleled opportunities for wildlife viewing and outdoor exploration.

One of the most iconic natural wonders of Southwest Florida is the Everglades, a vast expanse of subtropical wetlands that serves as a haven for an astonishing diversity of flora and fauna. Here, visitors can embark on airboat tours or guided hikes to discover elusive creatures such as alligators, wading birds, and endangered species like the

Florida panther and the West Indian manatee.

The coastal habitats of Southwest Florida are equally impressive, boasting miles of pristine beaches, mangrove forests, and estuaries that provide critical breeding grounds and foraging areas for marine life. Visitors can explore the unique ecosystems of places like Ding Darling National Wildlife Refuge on Sanibel Island or Lovers Key State Park near Fort Myers Beach, where they may encounter dolphins, sea turtles, and a myriad of bird species.

Barrier islands such as Sanibel, Captiva, and Gasparilla Island are renowned for their abundance of seashells, attracting shell enthusiasts from around the world. These islands also offer opportunities for shelling, kayaking, and wildlife watching, making them popular destinations for nature lovers and outdoor enthusiasts.

In addition to its coastal and wetland habitats, Southwest Florida is also home to unique upland ecosystems such as pine flatwoods, hardwood hammocks, and scrub habitats. These areas provide habitat for a variety of species, including the elusive Florida scrub-jay and the gopher tortoise.

The region's biodiversity extends beyond its terrestrial and aquatic ecosystems to include its vibrant coral reefs and seagrass beds, which support an array of marine life, including colorful reef fish, sea turtles, and manatees. Snorkeling and diving enthusiasts can explore these underwater wonderlands off the coast of places like Naples, Marco Island, and the Florida Keys.

Overall, Southwest Florida's biodiversity and natural wonders offer endless opportunities for exploration and discovery, whether you're a nature enthusiast, wildlife photographer, or simply someone who appreciates the beauty and splendor of the natural world. From the mangrove-lined estuaries to the crystal-clear waters of the Gulf of Mexico, the region's diverse landscapes and ecosystems are waiting to be explored and cherished for generations to come.

Chapter Two: Exploring Coastal Gems

Gulf Coast Beaches

The Gulf Coast of Florida boasts some of the most stunning beaches in the United States, particularly in the southwest region. From the serene shores of Sanibel Island to the vibrant atmosphere of Siesta Key, each beach offers a unique experience for visitors. Here's a detailed overview of some of the top Gulf Coast beaches in southwest Florida:

1. Siesta Key Beach: Consistently ranked as one of the best beaches in the world, Siesta Key Beach is famous for its powdery white sand, which is composed of 99% pure quartz. The soft sand stays cool even on the hottest days, making it ideal for lounging and sunbathing. The beach is also popular for its clear turquoise waters, perfect for swimming, snorkeling, and other water activities. Amenities include picnic areas, volleyball courts, and concession stands.

2. Naples Beach: Located in the charming city of Naples, this beach offers a tranquil escape with its pristine shoreline and breathtaking sunsets. Visitors can stroll along the historic Naples Pier, go shelling along the coast, or simply relax and soak up the sun. The beach is also known for its cleanliness and well-maintained facilities, including restrooms, showers, and parking.

3. Sanibel Island Beaches: Sanibel Island is renowned for its abundance of seashells, making it a paradise for shell collectors. The beaches here, such as Bowman's Beach and Lighthouse Beach, are known for their natural beauty and abundant wildlife. Visitors can explore nature trails, go birdwatching, or try their hand at fishing. Sanibel Island is also famous for its laid-back atmosphere and charming beachfront cottages.

4. Fort Myers Beach: With its lively atmosphere and wide range of activities, Fort Myers Beach is a favorite destination for families and thrill-seekers alike. The beach stretches for seven miles along Estero Island and offers opportunities for swimming, jet-skiing, parasailing, and more. The bustling Times Square area is lined with shops, restaurants, and entertainment options, ensuring there's never a dull moment.

5. Captiva Island Beaches: Just north of Sanibel Island lies the enchanting Captiva Island, known for its romantic sunsets and picturesque beaches. Visitors can enjoy kayaking through the mangrove forests, exploring the charming village of Captiva, or simply relaxing on the soft sandy shores. South Seas Island Resort offers access to some of the island's most secluded beaches, perfect for those seeking tranquility.

6. Anna Maria Island Beaches: This laid-back barrier island is home to pristine beaches, quaint beachfront cottages, and a relaxed vibe. Anna Maria Island boasts several stunning beaches, including Bean Point, Coquina Beach, and Manatee Public Beach. Visitors can enjoy swimming, fishing, kayaking, or simply unwinding with a beachfront picnic. The island's charming shops and restaurants add to its appeal.

7. Lido Key Beach: Situated just off the coast of Sarasota, Lido Key Beach offers a mix of natural beauty and urban amenities. The beach is known for its fine white sand, clear blue waters, and stunning views of the Gulf of Mexico. Visitors can swim, snorkel, or explore the nearby mangrove tunnels at Ted Sperling Park. St. Armands Circle, located nearby, is a popular shopping and dining destination.

These are just a few highlights of the Gulf Coast beaches in southwest Florida. Whether you're seeking relaxation, adventure, or natural beauty, you'll find it all along this picturesque coastline.

Barrier Islands and Key Attractions

Southwest Florida is blessed with a string of barrier islands that dot its coastline, each offering a unique blend of natural beauty, outdoor adventures, and cultural attractions.

Here's an in-depth look at some of the barrier islands and key attractions in the region:

1. Sanibel Island: Known for its world-class shelling beaches, Sanibel Island is a haven for nature lovers and beachgoers alike. The J.N. "Ding" Darling National Wildlife Refuge is a must-visit, offering opportunities for birdwatching, kayaking, and wildlife photography. The island's quaint shops, art galleries, and restaurants along Periwinkle Way provide plenty of entertainment options.

2. Captiva Island: Connected to Sanibel by a bridge, Captiva Island offers a more secluded and upscale atmosphere. Visitors can explore the charming Captiva Village, known for its colorful cottages and vibrant art scene. Sunset cruises departing from

Captiva are a popular way to experience the island's breathtaking sunsets over the Gulf of Mexico.

3. Marco Island: The largest of the Ten Thousand Islands, Marco Island is known for its pristine beaches, lush mangrove forests, and abundant wildlife. Tigertail Beach is a favorite spot for beachcombing and birdwatching, while South Marco Beach offers opportunities for watersports such as paddleboarding and jet-skiing. The island's upscale resorts and golf courses cater to luxury travelers.

4. Naples: While not technically an island, Naples is surrounded by barrier islands such as Keewaydin Island and Marco Island. The city itself boasts upscale shopping districts, fine dining establishments, and cultural attractions like the Naples Botanical Garden and the Naples Pier. Nearby Delnor-Wiggins Pass State Park is known for its unspoiled beaches and excellent fishing.

5. Anna Maria Island: This charming barrier island is known for its laid-back atmosphere, pristine beaches, and quaint beachfront cottages. Key attractions include the Historic Anna Maria City Pier, where visitors can fish and watch for dolphins, and the Anna Maria Island Historical Society Museum, which showcases the island's rich history and heritage.

6. Longboat Key: Stretching for 12 miles between Sarasota Bay and the Gulf of Mexico, Longboat Key offers a mix of luxury resorts, championship golf courses, and pristine beaches. Visitors can enjoy kayaking through the mangrove tunnels at Joan M. Durante Park or exploring the upscale shops and restaurants along St. Armands Circle.

7. Lido Key: Just off the coast of Sarasota, Lido Key is known for its beautiful beaches, upscale resorts, and vibrant arts scene. St. Armands Circle is the island's main attraction, featuring boutique shops, art galleries, and gourmet restaurants. Lido Key Beach is a popular spot for swimming, sunbathing, and sunset watching.

These are just a few of the barrier islands and key attractions that make southwest Florida a sought-after destination for travelers seeking sun, sand, and outdoor adventure. Whether you're exploring the natural wonders of Sanibel Island or indulging in the luxury of Marco Island, there's something for everyone to enjoy along this picturesque coastline.

Coastal Activities and Water Sports

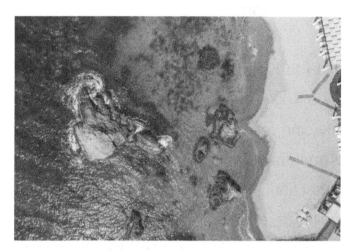

Southwest Florida's coastal region offers a plethora of activities and water sports for visitors of all ages and interests. From adrenaline-pumping adventures to leisurely pursuits, there's something for everyone to enjoy along this picturesque coastline. Here's an extensive overview of coastal activities and water sports in the region:

1. Boating: With its numerous bays, estuaries, and mangrove-lined waterways, southwest Florida is a boater's paradise. Visitors can rent boats, kayaks, or paddleboards to explore the region's pristine waterways at their own pace. Popular boating destinations include the Ten Thousand Islands, Charlotte Harbor, and the Intracoastal Waterway.

2. Fishing: Southwest Florida offers some of the best fishing opportunities in the state, thanks to its diverse ecosystems and abundant marine life. Anglers can try their luck at catching snook, redfish, tarpon, and other prized game fish in the Gulf of Mexico or the region's inland waterways. Deep-sea fishing charters depart from ports such as Naples, Fort Myers, and Sarasota, offering anglers the chance to reel in big game species like grouper and kingfish.

3. Jet Skiing: For those seeking thrills on the water, jet skiing is a popular activity along southwest Florida's coastline. Visitors can rent jet skis from various outfitters and explore the region's waterways while enjoying the exhilarating sensation of speeding across the waves. Many rental companies offer guided tours, allowing participants to discover hidden coves, mangrove forests, and scenic islands.

4. Parasailing: Take to the skies and enjoy breathtaking views of the Gulf Coast with a parasailing adventure. Parasailing operators in cities like Fort Myers Beach, Marco Island, and Sarasota offer tandem rides, allowing participants to soar above the water while securely attached to a parachute towed by a boat. It's an unforgettable way to experience the beauty of the coastline from a unique perspective.

5. Snorkeling and Scuba Diving: Explore the vibrant underwater world of southwest Florida's coral reefs, artificial reefs, and shipwrecks with a snorkeling or scuba diving excursion. Popular dive sites include the coral reefs of the Florida Keys National Marine Sanctuary, the sunken USS Mohawk off the coast of Sanibel Island, and the artificial reefs of Sarasota County. Guided tours and certification courses are available for both beginners and experienced divers.

6. Stand-up Paddleboarding (SUP): SUP has become increasingly popular along southwest Florida's coastline, offering a fun and relaxing way to explore the region's waterways. Visitors can rent paddleboards from beachside vendors and navigate the calm waters of bays, lagoons, and estuaries while enjoying views of the surrounding scenery and wildlife. Many outfitters also offer guided SUP tours, including sunrise and sunset excursions.

7. Beachcombing and Shelling: Southwest Florida's beaches are renowned for their abundance of seashells, making beachcombing a favorite pastime for visitors of all ages. Popular shelling beaches include Sanibel Island, Captiva Island, and Marco Island, where collectors can find an array of colorful shells, sand dollars, and other treasures washed ashore by the Gulf currents.

8. Sailing: Whether you're a seasoned sailor or a novice looking to learn the ropes, southwest Florida offers excellent sailing opportunities for all skill levels. Sailboat rentals, charters, and sailing lessons are available in marinas and yacht clubs throughout the region, allowing visitors to experience the thrill of harnessing the wind and navigating the open waters of the Gulf Coast.

These are just a few examples of the many coastal activities and water sports available in southwest Florida. Whether you're seeking adventure, relaxation, or simply a connection with nature, you'll find plenty of opportunities to enjoy the region's beautiful coastline and pristine waters.

Chapter Three: Immersive Cultural Experiences

Historic Sites and Museums

Southwest Florida is rich in history, with a variety of historic sites and museums that offer visitors a glimpse into the region's past. From ancient Native American settlements to Spanish colonial forts and pioneer villages, there's much to explore and learn about in this culturally diverse area. Here's a detailed overview of some of the notable historic sites and museums in southwest Florida:

1. Edison and Ford Winter Estates (Fort Myers): This iconic historic site preserves the winter homes of two American innovators, Thomas Edison and Henry Ford. Visitors can explore the beautifully preserved estates, including the Edison Botanic Research Laboratory and the Ford House. The site also features botanical gardens, a museum showcasing the inventors' contributions, and guided tours highlighting their legacies.

2. Sanibel Historical Village and Museum (Sanibel Island): Step back in time at the Sanibel Historical Village, a living history museum that recreates life on Sanibel Island from the late 19th to early 20th centuries. The village features a collection of historic buildings, including a schoolhouse, a pioneer cottage, and a general store, furnished with period artifacts and exhibits. Guided tours offer insights into the island's pioneer settlers and early industries.

3. Southwest Florida Museum of History (Fort Myers): Housed in the former Atlantic Coastline Railroad Depot, this museum showcases the history and cultural heritage of southwest Florida. Exhibits cover a range of topics, including Native American artifacts, Spanish exploration, pioneer settlements, and the region's role in the Civil War and World War II. Interactive displays and multimedia presentations provide an engaging learning experience for visitors of all ages.

4. Collier County Museums (Naples): The Collier County Museums system encompasses several historic sites and museums that celebrate the history and heritage of the region. Key attractions include the Naples Depot Museum, which explores the area's transportation history, and the Museum of the Everglades, which highlights the impact of the Tamiami Trail on the development of southwest Florida. Other sites include the Marco Island Historical Museum and the Immokalee Pioneer Museum at Roberts Ranch.

5. Mound Key Archaeological State Park (Estero Bay): Located in Estero Bay,

Mound Key is the site of an ancient Calusa Indian ceremonial center dating back over 2,000 years. Visitors can explore the shell mounds, canals, and other archaeological features left behind by the Calusa civilization. The park is accessible only by boat, making it a unique destination for history enthusiasts and outdoor adventurers alike.

6. Ringling Museum of Art (Sarasota): While technically located outside of southwest Florida, the Ringling Museum of Art is a must-visit attraction for those interested in history and culture. The museum, part of the Ringling estate built by circus magnate John Ringling, features a vast collection of European and American art, including works by Old Masters such as Rubens, Velázquez, and Titian. The estate also includes the Ca' d'Zan mansion, the

Circus Museum, and beautifully landscaped gardens.

7. Boca Grande Lighthouse Museum (Gasparilla Island): Perched on the southern tip of Gasparilla Island, the Boca Grande Lighthouse is a historic landmark dating back to the late 19th century. The museum located within the lighthouse keeper's cottage offers exhibits on the area's maritime history, including the role of the lighthouse in guiding ships through the treacherous waters of Charlotte Harbor and the Gulf of Mexico.

These are just a few examples of the historic sites and museums that showcase the rich cultural heritage of southwest Florida. Whether you're interested in pioneer history, Native American archaeology, or the legacies of famous inventors, you'll find plenty to explore and discover in this fascinating region.

Art Galleries and Cultural Festivals

Southwest Florida boasts a vibrant arts scene, with numerous art galleries and cultural festivals that showcase the talents of local and international artists alike. From contemporary art to traditional crafts, there's something for every art enthusiast to enjoy in this culturally rich region. Here's a detailed overview of some of the top art galleries and cultural festivals in southwest Florida:

Art Galleries:

1. Artis—Naples (Naples): Formerly known as The Philharmonic Center for the Arts, Artis—Naples is a premier cultural destination that includes a performing arts hall, a sculpture garden, and an art museum. The museum features rotating exhibitions of contemporary and classical art, including works by renowned artists from around the world.

2. Naples Art Association (Naples): Established in 1954, the Naples Art Association promotes visual arts education and appreciation through exhibitions, classes, and community outreach programs. The association operates a gallery in

downtown Naples that showcases works by local and regional artists in a variety of media, including painting, sculpture, photography, and mixed media.

3. Sidney & Berne Davis Art Center (Fort Myers): Housed in a historic building in downtown Fort Myers, the Sidney & Berne Davis Art Center is a cultural hub that hosts art exhibitions, performances, and special events throughout the year. The center features galleries showcasing contemporary art, as well as studio spaces for resident artists.

4. Hodges University Gallery of Art (Naples): Located on the campus of Hodges University, the Gallery of Art showcases works by students, faculty, and visiting artists. The gallery features rotating exhibitions of painting, sculpture,

photography, and other media, providing a platform for emerging artists to showcase their talents.

5. Center for Visual Arts Bonita Springs (Bonita Springs): The Center for Visual Arts Bonita Springs is a nonprofit organization dedicated to promoting visual arts education and appreciation in the community. The center operates a gallery that hosts exhibitions of contemporary art by local, national, and international artists, as well as art classes, workshops, and special events.

Cultural Festivals:

1. Naples National Art Festival (Naples): Organized by the Naples Art Association,

the Naples National Art Festival is a juried fine art and craft show that attracts artists from across the country. Held annually in February, the festival features a wide range of artwork, including painting, sculpture, ceramics, jewelry, and photography.

2. ArtFest Fort Myers (Fort Myers): Celebrating its 20th anniversary in 2024, ArtFest Fort Myers is a premier art festival that takes place in downtown Fort Myers each February. The festival features works by more than 200 artists from around the country, as well as live music, food vendors, and interactive art experiences for visitors of all ages.

3. Bonita Springs National Art Festival (Bonita Springs): Held three times a year in January, February, and March, the Bonita Springs National Art Festival showcases fine

art and crafts by artists from across the country. The festival takes place at the Promenade at Bonita Bay and features a wide range of artwork, including painting, sculpture, jewelry, and photography.

4. Sarasota Art & Craft Festival (Sarasota): Hosted by the Sarasota Downtown Merchants Association, the Sarasota Art & Craft Festival is a juried outdoor art show featuring works by local and regional artists. The festival takes place in downtown Sarasota and includes live music, food vendors, and children's activities in addition to the art exhibits.

5. Englewood Fine Arts Festival (Englewood): Organized by the Englewood Arts Center, the Englewood Fine Arts Festival is an annual event that showcases the work of local and regional artists. The

festival features a wide range of artwork, including painting, sculpture, ceramics, jewelry, and fiber arts, as well as live music, food vendors, and children's activities.

These are just a few examples of the art galleries and cultural festivals that contribute to the vibrant arts scene in southwest Florida. Whether you're a seasoned art collector or simply appreciate creativity and craftsmanship, you'll find plenty to explore and enjoy in this culturally rich region.

Culinary Delights and Local Cuisine

Southwest Florida is a culinary paradise, offering a diverse range of culinary delights and local cuisine that reflect the region's rich cultural heritage and abundant natural resources. From fresh seafood and tropical fruits to international flavors and fusion cuisine, there's something to satisfy every palate in this food lover's haven. Here's a detailed overview of some of the culinary delights and local cuisine you can experience in southwest Florida:

1. Fresh Seafood: With its prime location along the Gulf of Mexico, southwest Florida is renowned for its fresh seafood offerings. Visitors can enjoy a variety of locally caught fish, including grouper, snapper, mahi-mahi, and stone crab. Popular seafood dishes include grouper sandwiches, shrimp and grits, seafood platters, and ceviche.

2. Key Lime Pie: No visit to southwest Florida is complete without indulging in a slice of Key lime pie. Made with tangy Key lime juice, sweetened condensed milk, and a graham cracker crust, this iconic dessert is a refreshing treat on a hot day. Many restaurants and bakeries in the region serve their own versions of this classic dessert, each with its own unique twist.

3. Stone Crab: Southwest Florida is famous for its stone crab harvest, which takes place from October to May each year. Stone crab claws are prized for their sweet, tender meat and are typically served chilled with a side of mustard sauce. Many seafood restaurants in the region offer stone crab as a seasonal delicacy when it's in season.

4. Cuban Cuisine: Southwest Florida has a strong Cuban influence, thanks to its proximity to Cuba and its history of Cuban immigration. Visitors can enjoy authentic Cuban dishes such as Cuban sandwiches, picadillo, ropa vieja, and plantain chips at local Cuban restaurants and eateries. Don't forget to try a refreshing mojito or cafecito to complete your Cuban dining experience.

5. Tropical Fruits: Southwest Florida's warm climate allows for the cultivation of a wide variety of tropical fruits, including mangoes, papayas, pineapples, and coconuts. Visitors can enjoy these fresh fruits in smoothies, salads, desserts, and cocktails at local restaurants and juice bars. Many farmers' markets in the region also sell fresh, locally grown tropical fruits for visitors to enjoy.

6. Everglades Cuisine: The unique ecosystem of the Florida Everglades has influenced the region's culinary traditions, resulting in dishes that feature ingredients such as alligator, frog legs, and swamp cabbage. Visitors can sample Everglades cuisine at local restaurants and seafood shacks, where dishes are often prepared with a blend of Cajun, Creole, and Southern flavors.

7. Fusion Cuisine: Southwest Florida's diverse population has led to the emergence of fusion cuisine, blending flavors and ingredients from various culinary traditions. Visitors can enjoy creative dishes that combine Asian, Latin American, Caribbean, and European influences at local restaurants and eateries. From sushi burritos to Thai-inspired tacos, there's no shortage of innovative fusion fare to explore in the region.

8. Craft Beer and Spirits: Southwest Florida has a thriving craft beer and spirits scene, with numerous breweries, distilleries, and craft cocktail bars to explore. Visitors can sample locally brewed beers, spirits, and cocktails made with fresh, locally sourced ingredients at tasting rooms, brewpubs, and bars throughout the region.

Many establishments also offer tours and tastings where visitors can learn about the brewing and distilling process firsthand.

These are just a few examples of the culinary delights and local cuisine that await visitors in southwest Florida. Whether you're craving fresh seafood, tropical fruits, Cuban classics, or innovative fusion fare, you'll find plenty of delicious options to satisfy your appetite in this diverse and flavorful region.

Chapter Four: Wildlife Encounters and Nature Reserves

Everglades National Park: Flora and Fauna

Everglades National Park, located in southwest Florida, is a unique and diverse ecosystem that is home to a wide variety of flora and fauna. Covering 1.5 million acres of wetlands, mangroves, sawgrass prairies, and hardwood hammocks, the park is the largest tropical wilderness of any kind in the United States and is designated as a UNESCO World Heritage Site. Here's a detailed overview of the flora and fauna you can find in Everglades National Park:

Flora:

1. Sawgrass: Sawgrass is the iconic plant of the Everglades, covering vast stretches of the park's landscape. Despite its sharp edges, sawgrass is an important habitat for many species of wildlife and helps regulate water flow through the ecosystem.

2. Mangroves: Mangrove forests are found along the park's coastlines and estuaries, providing vital habitat for marine life and serving as a buffer against storm surges and erosion. The three main species of

mangroves found in the Everglades are red mangrove, black mangrove, and white mangrove.

3. Cypress Trees: Cypress trees can be found in the park's freshwater sloughs and swamps, where they thrive in the wet conditions. These majestic trees provide habitat for birds, mammals, and reptiles, and their knees (protrusions from the roots) help stabilize the soil.

4. Orchids and Bromeliads: The Everglades is home to a variety of orchids and bromeliads, including the ghost orchid, which is one of the park's most famous and elusive plants. These epiphytic plants grow on trees and other surfaces, adding color and beauty to the landscape.

5. Saw Palmetto: Saw palmetto is a common understory plant in the Everglades, forming dense thickets in some areas. The plant provides food and shelter for a variety of wildlife, including birds, insects, and small mammals.

6. Water Lilies: Water lilies and other aquatic plants can be found in the park's freshwater marshes and ponds, adding splashes of color to the landscape. These plants provide habitat for fish, amphibians, and waterfowl.

Fauna:

1. Alligators: The Everglades is home to a large population of American alligators, which can be found throughout the park's wetlands and waterways. These apex predators play a crucial role in the ecosystem by controlling populations of

smaller animals and helping to maintain the balance of the food chain.

2. Birds: The Everglades is a haven for birdwatchers, with over 360 species of birds recorded within the park. Common sightings include wading birds such as herons, egrets, and ibises, as well as birds of prey like ospreys and bald eagles.

3. Manatees: The park's coastal waters provide important habitat for West Indian manatees, which are often spotted in the park's estuaries and mangrove forests. These gentle giants are protected by federal and state laws due to their endangered status.

4. Panthers: The Florida panther, a subspecies of the cougar, is a rare and elusive resident of the Everglades. Although

sightings are rare, efforts to protect and conserve this iconic big cat are ongoing within the park.

5. Snakes: The Everglades is home to a variety of snake species, including the invasive Burmese python, which has become a major ecological concern in recent years. Native species such as the eastern diamondback rattlesnake and the cottonmouth are also found within the park.

6. Fish and Amphibians: The park's freshwater marshes and wetlands support a diverse array of fish and amphibian species, including largemouth bass, catfish, bullfrogs, and American alligator.

These are just a few examples of the diverse flora and fauna that call Everglades National Park home. Whether you're exploring the park's wetlands by airboat, hiking through its hammocks and pinelands, or paddling its waterways by kayak, you're sure to encounter an abundance of wildlife and natural beauty in this unique and ecologically important ecosystem.

Wildlife Refuges and Bird Watching

Southwest Florida boasts a rich and diverse ecosystem, making it a haven for wildlife enthusiasts and bird watchers alike. Here's an in-depth overview of wildlife refuges and bird-watching opportunities in the region:

1. J.N. "Ding" Darling National Wildlife Refuge:

- Located on Sanibel Island, this refuge is renowned for its bird-watching opportunities.

- Home to over 245 species of birds, including roseate spoonbills, herons, egrets, and ospreys.

- Visitors can explore the refuge via the Wildlife Drive, a scenic route that winds through mangrove forests, marshes, and tidal flats.

- The Visitor & Education Center offers interactive exhibits, guided tours, and educational programs.

2. Corkscrew Swamp Sanctuary:

- Situated near Naples, this sanctuary is one of the largest remaining stands of ancient bald cypress in North America.

- Bird watchers flock here to spot elusive species such as the wood stork, limpkin, and painted bunting.

- The 2.25-mile boardwalk meanders through diverse habitats, including wet prairies, pine flatwoods, and cypress swamps.

- Visitors can also participate in guided walks, birding tours, and educational programs led by knowledgeable naturalists.

3. Everglades National Park:

- While not exclusively in southwest Florida, Everglades National Park is easily accessible from the region and offers unparalleled wildlife viewing opportunities.

- Bird watchers can spot a wide array of species, including the elusive snail kite, the majestic American bald eagle, and the colorful roseate spoonbill.

- Popular birding hotspots within the park include Shark Valley, Anhinga Trail, and the Flamingo area.

- In addition to bird watching, visitors can enjoy airboat tours, hiking, biking, and ranger-led programs.

4. Estero Bay Preserve State Park:

- This coastal preserve, located near Fort Myers Beach, is a prime spot for bird watching and wildlife viewing.

- Bird enthusiasts can observe shorebirds, wading birds, and raptors along the park's trails and estuarine habitats.

- Kayaking and paddleboarding are popular activities for exploring the park's mangrove-lined waterways and spotting wildlife such as dolphins and manatees.

5. Caloosahatchee Regional Park:

- Nestled along the Caloosahatchee River in Alva, this park offers birding opportunities in a natural, unspoiled setting.

- Visitors can hike or bike along scenic trails through pine flatwoods, oak hammocks, and freshwater marshes.

- Bird watchers may encounter species such as the swallow-tailed kite, red-shouldered hawk, and barred owl.

6. Charlotte Harbor Preserve State Park:

- Located along the Charlotte Harbor estuary, this state park comprises diverse habitats, including mangrove forests, salt marshes, and tidal flats.

- Bird watchers can spot migratory shorebirds, waterfowl, and birds of prey while exploring the park's trails and waterways.

- Kayaking, canoeing, and fishing are popular activities for experiencing the park's natural beauty and wildlife.

7. Six Mile Cypress Slough Preserve:

- Situated in Fort Myers, this 3,500-acre wetland preserve is a haven for bird watchers and nature enthusiasts.

- The boardwalk trail winds through a cypress swamp, providing opportunities to observe a variety of bird species, including herons, ibises, and warblers.

- Interpretive signs along the trail offer insights into the preserve's ecology and wildlife.

When visiting these wildlife refuges and parks, it's essential to respect the natural environment and adhere to park regulations to ensure the protection of the area's wildlife and habitats. Additionally, consider bringing binoculars, a field guide, and comfortable walking shoes to enhance your bird-watching experience.

Eco-Tours and Nature Trails

Certainly Southwest Florida offers a plethora of eco-tours and nature trails for enthusiasts to immerse themselves in the region's diverse ecosystems. Here's an extensive overview:

1. Everglades National Park:

- While not exclusively in southwest Florida, Everglades National Park is easily accessible from the region and offers a range of eco-tours and nature trails.

- Visitors can embark on guided boat tours, kayak excursions, and tram rides to explore the park's wetlands, mangrove forests, and sawgrass prairies.

- Nature trails like Anhinga Trail and Shark Valley Loop provide opportunities for wildlife viewing, including alligators, wading birds, and elusive panthers.

- Ranger-led programs offer insights into the park's unique ecosystem and cultural history.

2. Corkscrew Swamp Sanctuary:

- Managed by the National Audubon Society, this sanctuary near Naples is renowned for its old-growth cypress forest and diverse wildlife.

- Visitors can explore a 2.25-mile boardwalk trail that winds through wet prairies, marshes, and the majestic cypress swamp.

- Guided walks led by experienced naturalists offer in-depth insights into the sanctuary's ecology, birdlife, and conservation efforts.

- Educational programs focus on topics such as wetland restoration, wildlife conservation, and bird identification.

3. Rookery Bay National Estuarine Research Reserve:

- Located in Naples, this reserve encompasses 110,000 acres of coastal mangroves, tidal flats, and protected waters.

- Eco-tours offer guided boat excursions through the reserve's estuarine habitats, providing opportunities to observe dolphins, manatees, and shorebirds.

- Kayak and paddleboard rentals allow visitors to explore the reserve's waterways at their own pace, immersing themselves in nature.

- The Environmental Learning Center features interactive exhibits, educational programs, and guided walks along nature trails.

4. Calusa Nature Center & Planetarium:

- Situated in Fort Myers, this nature center offers a variety of educational programs, exhibits, and nature trails.

- Visitors can explore over 100 acres of pine flatwoods, oak hammocks, and cypress swamps via self-guided nature trails.

- The Butterfly House showcases native butterfly species in a natural habitat, providing a unique opportunity for up-close observation.

- Educational programs cover topics such as native wildlife, environmental conservation, and astronomy.

5. Six Mile Cypress Slough Preserve:

- Located in Fort Myers, this 3,500-acre wetland preserve offers a tranquil escape into nature.

- The boardwalk trail winds through a cypress swamp, providing opportunities to observe a variety of wildlife, including herons, turtles, and otters.

- Interpretive signs along the trail offer insights into the preserve's ecology, hydrology, and wildlife habitats.

- Guided nature walks led by knowledgeable volunteers provide additional learning opportunities for visitors of all ages.

6. Estero Bay Preserve State Park:

- This coastal preserve near Fort Myers Beach offers a network of nature trails through diverse coastal habitats.

- Visitors can hike or bike along trails that traverse mangrove forests, salt marshes, and coastal dunes, providing opportunities for bird watching and wildlife viewing.

- Interpretive signs along the trails offer information about the park's natural and cultural history, including its importance as a habitat for endangered species.

7. Charlotte Harbor Preserve State Park:

- Situated along the Charlotte Harbor estuary, this state park offers scenic nature trails and paddling trails for outdoor enthusiasts.

- Hiking trails wind through diverse habitats, including mangrove forests, salt marshes, and coastal hammocks, providing opportunities for bird watching and wildlife observation.

- Paddling trails allow visitors to explore the park's waterways by kayak or canoe, providing opportunities to observe marine life and shorebirds.

When embarking on eco-tours and nature trails in southwest Florida, it's important to follow Leave No Trace principles, respect wildlife and natural habitats, and adhere to any posted regulations to ensure the protection of the region's fragile ecosystems. Additionally, consider joining guided tours or educational programs led by knowledgeable naturalists to enhance your experience and understanding of the area's natural wonders.

Chapter Five: Urban Escapes and Entertainment

Vibrant City Life: Sarasota and Naples

Sarasota and Naples, located in southwest Florida, offer vibrant city life with a unique blend of cultural richness, natural beauty, and modern amenities. Here's a detailed overview of both cities:

Sarasota:

1. Cultural Hub: Sarasota is renowned for its thriving arts scene, highlighted by the John and Mable Ringling Museum of Art, which boasts an impressive collection of Baroque art and is set within a stunning waterfront estate. The Sarasota Opera, Sarasota Ballet, and Sarasota Orchestra contribute to the city's cultural vibrancy.

2. Beaches: The city is blessed with beautiful beaches, including Siesta Key Beach, often ranked as one of the best beaches in the United States for its powdery white sand and crystal-clear waters. Lido Key and Longboat Key offer additional options for beachgoers.

3. Dining and Shopping: Sarasota offers a diverse culinary scene, with a plethora of restaurants ranging from upscale dining

establishments to casual beachside cafes. St. Armands Circle is a popular destination for shopping and dining, featuring boutique shops and restaurants in a charming European-style setting.

4. Outdoor Activities: Nature enthusiasts can explore the scenic beauty of Sarasota through activities such as kayaking in the mangrove tunnels of South Lido Nature Park, hiking in Myakka River State Park, or birdwatching at the Celery Fields.

5. Arts and Entertainment: Sarasota hosts numerous cultural events throughout the year, including the Sarasota Film Festival, Sarasota Music Festival, and Sarasota Improv Festival. The Van Wezel Performing Arts Hall attracts top performers from around the world.

6. Real Estate: Sarasota offers a wide range of housing options, from waterfront estates and luxury condominiums to historic homes in charming neighborhoods like Laurel Park and Gillespie Park. The city's real estate market is dynamic, with demand driven by its desirable location and quality of life.

Naples:

1. Luxury Living: Naples is renowned for its upscale lifestyle, featuring pristine beaches, championship golf courses, and luxury shopping destinations such as Fifth Avenue South and Waterside Shops. The city is known for its affluent residents and luxurious waterfront properties.

2. Golfing: Golf enthusiasts flock to Naples to experience its world-class golf courses, including Tiburón Golf Club, home to the PGA Tour's QBE Shootout, and The Old

Collier Golf Club, consistently ranked among the top courses in the country.

3. Cultural Attractions: Naples offers a rich cultural scene, with institutions such as The Baker Museum at Artis—Naples, which showcases a diverse collection of contemporary and modern art. The Naples Players and Gulfshore Playhouse provide high-quality theatrical performances year-round.

4. Dining and Cuisine: The dining scene in Naples is characterized by a mix of international cuisines and fresh seafood offerings. Waterfront restaurants like The Dock at Crayton Cove and Baleen Naples offer stunning views and delectable cuisine.

5. Natural Beauty: Naples boasts breathtaking natural beauty, with pristine

beaches, lush parks, and the stunning landscapes of nearby attractions like Everglades National Park and Corkscrew Swamp Sanctuary. Residents and visitors alike can enjoy outdoor activities such as boating, fishing, and wildlife viewing.

6. Real Estate: Naples offers an array of luxury real estate options, including beachfront estates, golf course communities, and exclusive gated neighborhoods like Port Royal and Pelican Bay. The city's real estate market is highly competitive, driven by demand from affluent buyers seeking upscale living experiences.

Overall, both Sarasota and Naples offer an unparalleled quality of life, combining cultural sophistication, outdoor recreation, and luxurious amenities amidst the natural beauty of southwest Florida. Whether you're drawn to Sarasota's vibrant arts scene or Naples' luxurious lifestyle, both cities provide an idyllic setting for residents and visitors alike.

Shopping and Dining Hotspots

In southwest Florida, there are numerous shopping and dining hotspots that cater to a diverse range of tastes and preferences. Here's a detailed overview of some of the top destinations:

Shopping Hotspots:

1. Waterside Shops (Naples): Located in Naples, Waterside Shops is an upscale outdoor shopping center featuring luxury brands such as Gucci, Louis Vuitton, and Tiffany & Co. The beautifully landscaped surroundings, along with fine dining options like Brio Tuscan Grille and BrickTop's, make it a premier shopping destination.

2. St. Armands Circle (Sarasota): This charming circular shopping district in Sarasota offers a mix of boutiques, galleries, and restaurants. Visitors can shop for unique gifts and apparel at stores like Lilly Pulitzer and Tommy Bahama, then dine at renowned eateries like Columbia Restaurant or Shore Diner.

3. Coconut Point (Estero): Situated in Estero, Coconut Point is a sprawling outdoor

mall with over 140 stores, including major retailers like Apple, H&M, and Dillard's. The center also features a variety of dining options, from casual eateries to upscale restaurants like Ruth's Chris Steak House.

4. Mercato (Naples): Mercato is a vibrant lifestyle center in Naples offering a mix of shopping, dining, and entertainment options. Visitors can explore trendy fashion boutiques, home decor stores, and specialty shops before enjoying a meal at one of the many restaurants, such as The Capital Grille or Bravo Cucina Italiana.

5. Gulf Coast Town Center (Fort Myers): Located in Fort Myers, Gulf Coast Town Center is a large outdoor shopping complex featuring over 100 stores, including anchor tenants like Bass Pro Shops and Belk. The

center also offers a diverse selection of dining options, ranging from fast-casual chains to sit-down restaurants.

Dining Hotspots:

1. 5th Avenue South (Naples): Known for its charming ambiance and diverse culinary scene, 5th Avenue South in Naples is lined with upscale restaurants, cafes, and wine bars. Visitors can indulge in everything from gourmet cuisine at The French Brasserie Rustique to authentic Italian fare at Barbatella.

2. Downtown Sarasota: Sarasota's downtown area is a foodie's paradise, with a wide range of dining options to suit every palate. From waterfront seafood restaurants like Marina Jack to trendy eateries such as

The Rosemary and Indigenous, there's no shortage of culinary delights to explore.

3. The Village Shops on Venetian Bay (Naples): Situated along the waterfront in Naples, The Village Shops on Venetian Bay offer picturesque views and an array of dining options. Visitors can dine al fresco at waterfront restaurants like M Waterfront Grille or enjoy casual fare at The Village Pub.

4. Bell Tower Shops (Fort Myers): Bell Tower Shops in Fort Myers is not only a shopping destination but also a hub for dining and entertainment. Visitors can choose from a variety of restaurants, including popular chains like T.G.I. Friday's and Blue Pointe Oyster Bar & Seafood Grill.

5. University Town Center (Sarasota): Located near the University of South Florida Sarasota-Manatee campus, University Town Center is a modern shopping and dining complex featuring a range of restaurants, from fast-casual options like Shake Shack to upscale eateries like The Cheesecake Factory.

These shopping and dining hotspots in southwest Florida offer something for everyone, whether you're in the mood for high-end shopping, casual dining, or gourmet cuisine. With their diverse offerings and vibrant atmospheres, they provide unforgettable experiences for residents and visitors alike.

Nightlife and Entertainment Venues

In southwest Florida, nightlife and entertainment venues cater to a diverse range of tastes, offering everything from vibrant clubs and bars to cultural performances and live music. Here's a detailed overview of some of the top destinations:

Nightlife Venues:

1. Ybor City (Tampa): While technically not in southwest Florida, Ybor City is a historic district in Tampa known for its lively nightlife scene. Visitors can explore numerous bars, clubs, and music venues along 7th Avenue, including the famous Columbia Restaurant and The RITZ Ybor.

2. Downtown Sarasota: Sarasota's downtown area comes alive at night with a variety of bars, pubs, and nightclubs catering to different tastes. From craft cocktail lounges like The Table Creekside to lively bars such as The Gator Club, there's something for everyone to enjoy.

3. Downtown Fort Myers: The River District in downtown Fort Myers offers a vibrant nightlife scene with a mix of bars, clubs, and entertainment venues. Visitors can dance

the night away at The Firestone or catch live music at The Barrel Room.

4. Mercato (Naples): Mercato in Naples transforms into a bustling nightlife hub after dark, with a variety of bars, restaurants, and entertainment options. Visitors can sip cocktails at Blue Martini or enjoy live music at Burn by Rocky Patel.

5. Gulf Coast Town Center (Fort Myers): While primarily a shopping destination, Gulf Coast Town Center also offers nightlife options such as World of Beer and Miller's Ale House, where visitors can enjoy a casual atmosphere and a wide selection of drinks.

Entertainment Venues:

1. Sarasota Opera House: As a cultural hub in Sarasota, the Sarasota Opera House hosts a variety of performances, including opera, musicals, and concerts. The historic venue's stunning architecture and world-class acoustics provide an unforgettable entertainment experience.

2. Artis—Naples: Located in Naples, Artis—Naples is home to the Baker Museum, which features a diverse collection of visual art, as well as the Naples Philharmonic, which offers classical music concerts and other performances throughout the year.

3. Van Wezel Performing Arts Hall: Situated along Sarasota's waterfront, the Van Wezel Performing Arts Hall hosts a wide range of performances, including Broadway shows, concerts, comedy acts, and dance performances. Its iconic purple architecture

makes it a recognizable landmark in the area.

4. Barbara B. Mann Performing Arts Hall: Located on the campus of Florida SouthWestern State College in Fort Myers, the Barbara B. Mann Performing Arts Hall hosts a variety of cultural performances, including Broadway musicals, symphony orchestra concerts, and comedy shows.

5. The Naples Players: The Naples Players is a community theater group in Naples that produces a diverse range of theatrical productions, including dramas, comedies, and musicals. Their performances take place at the Sugden Community Theatre in downtown Naples.

These nightlife and entertainment venues in southwest Florida offer residents and visitors alike a multitude of options for enjoying evenings out on the town, whether it's dancing the night away at a club, catching a live performance, or sipping cocktails at a chic lounge. With their diverse offerings and lively atmospheres, they contribute to the region's vibrant cultural scene.

Chapter Six: Practical Information

Transportation and Getting Around

In southwest Florida, transportation options are diverse, ranging from traditional modes like cars and buses to more unconventional methods like water taxis. Here's a detailed overview of transportation and getting around in the region:

1. Cars:

- Personal Vehicles: Like much of the United States, personal vehicles are the primary mode of transportation for residents in southwest Florida. Major highways such as Interstate 75 (I-75) and Tamiami Trail (U.S. Route 41) provide convenient access to key destinations within the region.

- Car Rentals: Visitors to southwest Florida can easily rent cars from various rental agencies located at airports and in major cities like Fort Myers, Sarasota, and Naples. This provides flexibility for exploring the region at one's own pace.

2. Public Transportation:

- Buses: The region is served by public bus systems operated by agencies such as Sarasota County Area Transit (SCAT), LeeTran in Lee County, and Collier Area Transit (CAT) in Collier County. These bus services connect major cities, neighborhoods, and popular destinations within the region.

- Trolleys: Some cities, such as Sarasota and Fort Myers, offer trolley services that provide convenient transportation within specific areas. These charming trolleys often cater to tourists and offer a fun way to explore local attractions.

3. Ridesharing:

- Uber and Lyft: Ridesharing services like Uber and Lyft are widely available in southwest Florida, providing convenient and flexible transportation options for residents and visitors alike. These services operate in major cities and tourist areas throughout the region.

4. Biking and Walking:

- Bike Lanes and Trails: Many cities in southwest Florida are bike-friendly, with designated bike lanes and trails that cater to cyclists of all levels. The Legacy Trail in Sarasota County and the Gordon River Greenway in Naples are popular routes for biking and walking.

- Pedestrian-Friendly Areas: Downtown areas such as Sarasota's Main Street and Naples' Fifth Avenue South are pedestrian-friendly, with sidewalks, crosswalks, and pedestrian-friendly amenities that encourage walking and exploration.

5. Water Transportation:

- Ferries and Water Taxis: In coastal areas like Sarasota and Naples, water transportation options such as ferries and water taxis provide a unique way to travel between islands, waterfront destinations, and coastal communities. These services offer scenic views and convenient access to popular attractions.

6. Air Travel:

- Airports: Southwest Florida is served by several airports, including Sarasota-Bradenton International Airport (SRQ), Southwest Florida International Airport (RSW) in Fort Myers, and Naples Municipal Airport (APF). These airports offer domestic and international flights, connecting the region to major cities and destinations worldwide.

7. Shuttle Services:

- Hotel Shuttles: Many hotels and resorts in southwest Florida offer complimentary shuttle services to nearby attractions, beaches, and airports. This convenient amenity allows guests to explore the area without the need for a car.

Overall, southwest Florida offers a range of transportation options to suit different preferences and needs. Whether by car, public transit, ridesharing, biking, walking, or water transportation, residents and visitors can navigate the region efficiently and enjoyably, experiencing all that southwest Florida has to offer.

Accommodation Options and Recommendations

In southwest Florida, accommodation options range from luxurious beachfront resorts to charming boutique hotels and cozy vacation rentals. Here's a detailed overview of accommodation options and recommendations in the region:

1. Beachfront Resorts:
   - The Ritz-Carlton, Naples: Situated on the pristine shores of the Gulf of Mexico, The Ritz-Carlton, Naples offers luxurious accommodations, world-class amenities,

and breathtaking ocean views. Guests can enjoy access to a private beach, multiple pools, spa services, and upscale dining options.

- The Ritz-Carlton, Sarasota: Located in downtown Sarasota, The Ritz-Carlton, Sarasota combines elegance with sophistication. This waterfront resort features spacious rooms, a championship golf course, a lavish spa, and dining options that highlight local flavors.

2. Luxury Hotels:

-The Inn on Fifth, Naples: Nestled in the heart of downtown Naples, The Inn on Fifth offers upscale accommodations with European-inspired décor. Guests can enjoy amenities such as a rooftop pool, complimentary beach transportation, and access to nearby shopping and dining.

- The Resort at Longboat Key Club: Situated on a barrier island between Sarasota Bay and the Gulf of Mexico, The Resort at Longboat Key Club offers luxury accommodations, championship golf courses, tennis courts, a spa, and multiple dining options.

3. Boutique Hotels:

- Hotel Indigo, Sarasota: Located in the Rosemary District of downtown Sarasota, Hotel Indigo offers stylish accommodations with a modern flair. Guests can enjoy amenities such as a rooftop pool, a fitness center, and a restaurant showcasing locally-sourced ingredients.

- Inn at Pelican Bay, Naples: This intimate boutique hotel in Naples offers comfortable accommodations surrounded by lush tropical landscaping. Guests can relax by the pool, take a complimentary shuttle to the beach, and enjoy a complimentary breakfast each morning.

4. Vacation Rentals:

- Airbnb and VRBO: Southwest Florida offers a wide range of vacation rental options through platforms like Airbnb and VRBO. From waterfront condos to beachfront cottages and spacious villas, travelers can find accommodations that suit their preferences and budget.

- Vacation Rental Agencies: Numerous vacation rental agencies in southwest Florida manage properties ranging from cozy beach bungalows to luxurious estates. These agencies provide personalized service and assistance in finding the perfect rental for your stay.

5. Budget-Friendly Options:

- Chain Hotels: Southwest Florida has several budget-friendly chain hotels and motels that offer comfortable accommodations at affordable rates. Options include brands like Holiday Inn Express, Hampton Inn, and Best Western.

- Bed and Breakfasts: For a charming and affordable stay, consider booking a room at a bed and breakfast in cities like Sarasota or Naples. These quaint establishments offer cozy accommodations and personalized service in a home-like setting.

6. RV Parks and Campgrounds:

- State Parks: Southwest Florida is home to several state parks with RV camping facilities, including Myakka River State Park and Lovers Key State Park. These parks offer scenic campsites surrounded by nature, with amenities such as restrooms, showers, and picnic areas.

- Private Campgrounds: Private campgrounds and RV parks throughout the region provide a range of amenities and facilities for campers, including full hook-up sites, swimming pools, laundry facilities, and recreational activities.

Whether you're seeking a luxurious beachfront retreat, a cozy boutique hotel, a spacious vacation rental, or a budget-friendly accommodation option, southwest Florida offers a diverse range of choices to suit every traveler's needs and preferences. With its stunning natural beauty, vibrant cultural scene, and array of attractions, southwest Florida provides the perfect backdrop for an unforgettable getaway.

Tips for Safe and Enjoyable Travel

Traveling in southwest Florida can be a memorable experience filled with sun-soaked beaches, vibrant culture, and abundant natural beauty. To ensure a safe and enjoyable trip, here are some detailed tips to keep in mind:

1. Weather Awareness:

  - Southwest Florida experiences a tropical climate, characterized by warm temperatures and frequent rain showers, especially during the summer months. Be prepared for sudden changes in weather and stay updated on local forecasts.

  - During hurricane season (June to November), monitor weather alerts and follow instructions from local authorities. Consider purchasing travel insurance to cover any potential disruptions to your trip.

2. Sun Protection:

- The Florida sun can be intense year-round. Protect yourself from sunburn and heat-related illnesses by wearing sunscreen with a high SPF, sunglasses, and a wide-brimmed hat. Drink plenty of water to stay hydrated, especially when spending time outdoors.

3. Water Safety:

- When swimming in the Gulf of Mexico or other bodies of water, be aware of potential hazards such as strong currents, rip currents, and marine life like jellyfish and stingrays. Swim at designated beaches with lifeguards on duty, and obey warning flags and signs.

4. Wildlife Awareness:

- Southwest Florida is home to diverse wildlife, including alligators, snakes, and various species of birds. Exercise caution when exploring natural areas and respect wildlife habitats. Do not approach or feed wild animals, and keep a safe distance at all times.

5. Bug Protection:

- Mosquitoes and other biting insects are prevalent in Florida, especially during the warmer months. Use insect repellent containing DEET or other EPA-approved ingredients to protect yourself from bites. Consider wearing long sleeves and pants, particularly during dusk and dawn when mosquitoes are most active.

6. Driving Safety:

- If renting a car, familiarize yourself with local traffic laws and regulations. Drive defensively, especially on busy highways and in urban areas. Be mindful of pedestrians and cyclists, and avoid distractions such as texting or using a mobile phone while driving.

7. Avoiding Wildlife Encounters:

- Be cautious when walking or hiking in natural areas, as encounters with wildlife like alligators and snakes are possible. Stay on designated trails, keep pets on a leash, and never approach or attempt to feed wild animals.

8. Hydration and Heat Safety:

- Florida's high temperatures and humidity levels can lead to heat-related illnesses such as heat exhaustion and heatstroke.

Stay hydrated by drinking plenty of water throughout the day, and take breaks in shaded or air-conditioned areas to cool down.

9. COVID-19 Precautions:

- Stay informed about COVID-19 guidelines and regulations in southwest Florida, including mask mandates, social distancing measures, and any travel restrictions in place. Follow recommended hygiene practices such as frequent handwashing and sanitizing, and adhere to any venue-specific protocols.

10. Emergency Preparedness:

- Familiarize yourself with the location of nearby hospitals, urgent care centers, and emergency services. Keep important contact information, including hotel addresses and local emergency numbers, readily accessible in case of an emergency.

By following these tips for safe and enjoyable travel in southwest Florida, you can make the most of your visit while minimizing potential risks and ensuring a memorable experience in this beautiful region.

Conclusion

In conclusion, traveling to southwest Florida offers a wealth of experiences for visitors seeking sun, sand, culture, and natural beauty. From the vibrant city life of Sarasota and Naples to the serene beaches of Sanibel Island and Captiva Island, the region captivates travelers with its diverse attractions and picturesque landscapes. Here's a detailed summary of what makes southwest Florida an unforgettable destination:

1. Natural Beauty: Southwest Florida boasts stunning beaches with powdery white sand and clear turquoise waters, making it a paradise for sunbathers, swimmers, and water sports enthusiasts. Beyond the beaches, the region is home to lush nature preserves, mangrove forests, and unique ecosystems teeming with wildlife.

2. Cultural Richness: Sarasota and Naples serve as cultural hubs, offering world-class museums, theaters, art galleries, and performing arts venues. Visitors can immerse themselves in the region's rich heritage through historical sites, festivals, and events celebrating local traditions and customs.

3. Outdoor Adventures: Whether kayaking through mangrove tunnels, exploring nature trails, or embarking on eco-tours, southwest Florida provides endless opportunities for outdoor adventure and exploration. From birdwatching in the Everglades to dolphin watching cruises along the Gulf Coast, nature lovers will find plenty to discover.

4. Gourmet Cuisine: Food enthusiasts will delight in southwest Florida's culinary scene, which features a diverse array of dining options ranging from fresh seafood shacks and waterfront cafes to upscale restaurants helmed by award-winning chefs. Local specialties such as stone crab claws, Gulf shrimp, and key lime pie showcase the region's coastal flavors and culinary creativity.

5. Luxurious Accommodations: Whether seeking a lavish beachfront resort, a charming boutique hotel, or a cozy vacation rental, southwest Florida offers accommodations to suit every taste and budget. From opulent amenities and personalized service to quaint bed and breakfasts and family-friendly resorts, visitors can find the perfect home base for their stay.

6. Safety and Convenience: Travelers can explore southwest Florida with confidence, knowing that safety measures and precautions are in place to protect visitors and residents alike. From well-maintained roads and public transportation systems to accessible healthcare facilities and emergency services, the region prioritizes the well-being and comfort of travelers.

In essence, traveling to southwest Florida offers a transformative experience filled with relaxation, adventure, and cultural immersion. Whether seeking a romantic getaway, a family vacation, or a solo adventure, the region welcomes visitors with open arms and endless possibilities for discovery. With its unparalleled beauty, rich heritage, and warm hospitality, southwest Florida invites travelers to create lifelong memories and cherish moments of joy and serenity in this enchanting corner of the Sunshine State.

Travel Planner

Destination (s)	When

Expenses	Budget	Actual

Transport ation		
Hotel		
Food		
Shopping		
Gifts		

113

Total		

Places to see

- _____

- _____

- _____

- _____

Places to eat

- _____

- _____

- _____

- _____

- _____

Places to shop

- _____

- _____

- _____

- _____

- _____

Emergency contacts

- _____

- _____

- _____

- _____

- _____

Addresses of places I'm staying at

- _____

- _____

- _____

- _____

Made in United States
North Haven, CT
20 January 2025

64645256R00070